Brother Lew
(Life or Death)

By Lou Acosta

Copyright April 2002
Lampara Music Publishing Group
P.O. Box 674
Lorain, Ohio 44055

Copyright © 2002 by Lou Acosta

Brother Lew
by Lou Acosta

Printed in the United States of America

Library of Congress Control Number: 2002103360
ISBN 1-591600-41-3

All rights reserved. No part of this publication may be reproduced or transmitted in any form or by any means without written permission of the publisher.

Xulon Press
11350 Random Hills Road
Suite 800
Fairfax, VA 22030
(703) 279-6511
XulonPress.com

To order additional copies, call 1-866-381-BOOK (2665).

Table of Contents

Author's Page 7
Personal Pre-Press Reviews 9
  1. My 'Hood 11
  2. Leaving Town 13
  3. A Greater Impact 15
  4. Left Holding the Bag 19
  5. Higher Education 23
  6. Rikers Island 27
  7. Reform School 31
  8. Revolving Door 33
  9. Bangin' 35
 10. Napanoch State Prison 39
 11. Music Was My Refuge 41
 12. In Da Mix 45
 13. Hit List 47
 14. Couldn't Handle It 53
 15. I Should Have Known Better 61
 16. Institutionalized? 65
 17. The Truth Will Set You Free 69
 18. Parole Anyone? 73
 19. Free at Last 79
 20. Seek Ye First 85
Photo Album 93

Author's Page

The story you are about to read is true to life. I've experienced so much drama in my life that I couldn't write it all down in one sitting. After receiving positive criticism from many people who read the short version of my testimony, I decided to write my book in a very simple format. In this book, I share some of the most painful times in my life, in the hope that those who are bound can be set free. I pray that when you have finished reading it, you will be blessed, inspired, and encouraged to go out and tell the world what God has done in your life. This book was produced for the purpose of outreach for the lost, evangelism for the needy, and encouragement for the body.

We encourage the body to use this book to reach out to people in jails, juvenile detention centers, prisons, rehab centers, hospices, hospitals, the armed forces, colleges, schools, or the streets. We must remember that tomorrow isn't promised to us, so let's reach out to the lost today, door-to-door, city-to-city, and nation-to-nation.

God bless you.

Personal Pre-Press Reviews

"All the men at this facility seemed to really enjoy reading it as I did" (Pat Strauss—Salvation Army/Harbor Light).

"The ladies couldn't put it down, and now they want more" (Holly Wade—Women's Director, Hanna House).

"Man, Lou, you need to put that testimony in Spanish, man. I'll help you pass it out all over Puerto Rico" (J.T.—Spanish Christian Rapper).

"Your testimony is like a Joseph Jennings or Nicky Cruz" (Mark Hebebrand—Youth Pastor, House of Praise International Church).

"I don't usually read a lot of books outside of the Bible, but after the first few pages, I couldn't put it down" (Grip—Christian Rapper).

"The Lord is definitely going to use you to reach masses of people" (Pastor Brian Wade—Director, Lorain County Mission).

"It was an awesome testimony" (Minister Elton Jones—Administrator, LCM).

"Lou's testimony was awesome. Now let's take an offering so that we can continue to bless his ministry" (Pastor Gilbert Silva—H.O.P. International).

"Man, I never knew that you went through so much. Awesome testimony" (Pastor Tim Geunther—Church of the Open Door).

"Lou's testimony was awesome. All the girls loved it" (Debbie—Resident, Hanna House for Women).

"Lou can reach over a million Hispanics with this testimony" (Jorge Valette—J-Squad, Spanish Christian Rapper).

CHAPTER 1

My 'Hood

Growing up in New York City helped to introduce me to the diverse cultures that surrounded the South Bronx: the people, the food, the music, the social classes, and their priorities.

My dear mother separated from my father when I was only eight years old. She said that she left him because he was a loan shark and a womanizer. She moved us to New York City, never to look back at that type of life again.

My neighborhood was mostly made up of Puerto Ricans. There were a few black families, but hardly any white folks except for the cops, the landlords, and the nuns that visited our neighborhood occasionally. The white folks that came into our neighborhood reminded me of missionaries, like the ones that I ministered with in Mexico, those who go into underdeveloped countries to help educate the populations there.

The only difference was that this was the South Bronx in New York City, in the United States of America. My favorite place to hang out in our little concrete jungle was on the rooftop of my building, which sat on the corner of 158th Street and St. Ann's Avenue in the Bronx.

The rooftop was my sanctuary, the one place where I could indulge in my number one passion: music. Whether I was listening to music, singing it, writing it, or playing my saxophone to it, it was an escape from the confines of my little world. I loved all types of music, especially Latin and oldies, but the Motown sound ruled my AM radio dial.

One thing that was very common in our neighborhood was domestic violence. People didn't talk about it much, as though it was not happening, but it was, especially in our own home.

In the daytime, the kids went to school and the parents worked, so you would rarely see many folks around our neighborhood. In the evening it was different—you could hear the sirens screaming, the tires screeching, the horns honking, and the people yelling.

Some of the games that I participated in when I wasn't chillin' on the rooftop were Ringolivio, Tag, Kick the Can, Johnnie on the Pony, Stickball, or a game called Skelzy. I wouldn't trade my neighborhood in for anything in the world—we had fun living there, and whatever the situation, the people in our neighborhood looked out for each other.

CHAPTER 2

Leaving Town

One of the saddest things that had happened in my neighborhood was when one of my classmates was killed by his stepfather. Alfonso, as he was known, was only seven years old when they found him hanging with a rope around his neck. The kids in our second grade class were very saddened that this had happened to someone we all knew.

Sometimes I would think about Alfonso and the situation in my own house. I would get nightmares about my stepfather or someone else who was trying to hurt me. I would remember those dreams most when I would have to confront him for hitting my mother. When my sister Luisa was born, the number in our family grew to five, and we knew that we had to get a bigger place to live. The following year, my stepfather took on a position as a building janitor and we moved into a predominantly Irish neighborhood.

In the summer of 1962, while living in this new neighborhood, I was playing with a friend named Danny Moran. About an hour later, his older brother Michael came home very upset. I started to leave for home, but Michael stopped me. He started cursing at me for being in his house, and as I tried to leave, he spun me around and punched me in the face. He was looking for someone to let out his frustrations on, and I happened to be at the wrong place at the wrong time. I ran home crying, but within a few minutes my stepfather brought me back to Michael's house. Michael stepped outside and my stepfather made me fight Michael Moran in the middle of the crowded street in our new neighborhood.

Not only did I lose the fight to a kid twice my size, but I got beat up by my stepfather for losing the fight to this Irishman. The pain, the hurt, and the embarrassment went away, but I couldn't understand why my stepfather didn't throw in the towel when I was losing. Instead, he went off on me and beat me like a stepchild.

Shortly after that incident, my stepfather realized that there were many more racist folks in the neighborhood who didn't like Puerto Ricans, so he took on a factory job and we moved out. For the first time in my life I realized that the color of my skin played a big part in whether I was accepted or rejected in certain parts of society.

CHAPTER 3

A Greater Impact

I was doing well in school, in sports and at home, but once my baby sister died, all of that changed. In the early morning hours of May 9, 1963, my mother woke me up to tell me that she was taking my younger sister Luisa to the hospital. Luisa had been throwing up blood before she was rushed out. When my mother came home by herself, without my baby sister, we knew that something was wrong. My baby sister Luisa had died of Leukemia.

From that time until the end of school, I had refused to eat very much or talk to hardly anyone. My mother didn't like what was happening to me, and she tried to convince me to go out and play with my friends.

A few months later that summer, I went outside to play stickball with my friends. We played in the middle of the street on Teller Avenue and 165th Street. It was about the third inning, and my friend Roberto threw me a pitch, I swung the bat to hit the ball, the catcher came in a little too close, and catastrophe hit. I took a full swing that spun me around until the bat hit the catcher's mouth. Even though I had hit the ball, I couldn't run. I couldn't move. I was paralyzed by what had just taken place. Ivan's teeth were flying everywhere, and he had blood all over his face. It wasn't long before the entire neighborhood was out on the street trying to calm down Ivan and his mother. He was finally taken into the house, and needless to say, I was grounded for the rest of that summer.

School had resumed for the fall quarter, and I was trying hard to immerse myself in schoolwork. I also tried to stay away from my stepfather so as not to get blamed for anything. A few months later, on November 22, 1963, President Kennedy was shot and killed. The nation mourned, but the media had a field day with the coverage. For weeks they kept showing the graphic shooting scenes of the deaths of both John F. Kennedy and his alleged assassin, Lee Harvey Oswald. Many people criticized the media's sensationalism of such a tragic episode, but sensationalizing was what the media was all about, with little regard for the feelings of those involved. That was the beginning of what we call shock media today.

A few months later, the media toned down a little and changed their focus to music, or at least to a new singing group from England named the Beatles. I first heard about the Beatles through the New York radio station WMCA when they sponsored a name-the-group contest.

I met a new classmate who had moved into our neighborhood. His name was Joe Perez. I immediately gave him the nickname Pie. Sometimes he and I would hang out at his house listening to music, and other times we would cut class and go to hookie parties. Pie was a good timbale percussionist who loved music. He was the one who introduced me to Latin jazz. We eventually started sponsoring our own hookie parties and invited people from the surrounding public schools. We did this until some of the girls from our school went home drunk and their parents set off a huge investigation.

A Greater Impact

Pie had to move away with his dad, and I was expelled from school. My mother was furious when she found out that I was expelled, but later she enrolled me at another public school a few blocks from where I lived. In the summer of 1965, my mother sent me to visit my Aunt Dora and Uncle Pablo Rivera in Lorain, Ohio. Of course, being from New York City, my cousin and I had to teach the Lorain folks all the latest dance steps. I had a good time and met a lot of nice people in Ohio, but I had to get back to the big city. It was almost as if I was missing something.

When I arrived back in New York, I realized that the people in Lorain had it good compared to the people living in the Bronx. The only thing that I didn't appreciate about Lorain was that it had only three TV stations. I found out that while I was away, my mother and stepfather had separated. Later on that winter, I was rushed to the hospital because of a ruptured appendix. I stayed in the hospital for two weeks dealing with the post-surgery pains, while taking daily doses of Morphine.

CHAPTER 4

Left Holding the Bag

One day, two of my friends went with me to shop for a pair of sneakers near the Fordham and Grand Concourse area of the Bronx. On our way to the store, we stopped by a newsstand to look at some magazines. As I was reading a magazine, I was frightened when I heard the newsstand lady scream. I noticed her pointing to my friend as he was running away with her change purse in his hand. I turned around and assured her that I would get it back for her.

I ran after my friend for almost two blocks and finally caught up to him. I tackled him with my body weight and we both hit the concrete. All of the coins spilled out of the purse and onto the sidewalk, but before we could pick them all up, we were surrounded by policemen with their guns pointed at us.

We were taken to the police station, and had to wait for our parents to come and sign us out. Both of my friends were released into their parents' custody, but there was no sign of my mother. Three hours later, my mother finally showed up, but instead of taking me home, she just turned around and walked out. I never forgot the words that came out of her mouth that day: "He's not my son; you can have him." Nothing that ever happened in my life had crushed me more than those words that day. That evening I was sent to the juvenile detention center at Spofford in the Bronx.

Later that evening, I started to look out the window on the fifth floor of the detention center, and that's when reality had set in. My mother wasn't coming to pick me up, and I wasn't going home. Then my tears started to pour out. As the hours passed, I realized that I was in this strange place for the duration. The longer I stared out the window, the more I knew that I had to get out of the place that very night. I looked out the window and measured the drop from the fifth floor to the third floor, and then to the 100-foot wall. I thought that if I could break the screen and the glass, then tie some bed sheets and let myself down onto the ledge of the third floor, I could probably walk along the side of the wall and jump off. The top of the wall off the third floor was at least 100 feet to the ground. It would be a suicide jump, but then who would care if I killed myself anyway? Didn't my own mother say that she disowned me?

I just couldn't believe that my mother would do this to me. I loved my mother so much that I was willing to be used as a punching bag by my stepfather so that she wouldn't get hit. I thought about my grandmother, who I believed was the only person who really loved me. I guess that thinking about her relaxed me a little, then the door to my room opened. The guard had brought in a new roommate. Both of us spent the rest of the evening hours talking about ourselves and the neighborhoods we came from.

By the next morning, I had forgotten all about my escape plans, especially when I saw some of my homeboys in the cafeteria. They all started talking about their individual cases, and then one of them asked me about my crime. I thought for a minute about my situation, and then I said "robbery." Everybody looked at me as though they knew I would be heading upstate. To think that twenty-four hours prior to that, I was about to jump out of a window and possibly get killed in the process.

Two weeks later, I went to court and saw my so-called accomplices, sitting with their parents while the newsstand lady was sitting on the witness chair. As I looked around for my mother in the crowded courtroom, I heard the newsstand clerk tell the judge that I was the one who was trying to help get her purse back. The judge looked surprised and said, "Are you trying to tell me that this young man was not the one who took your change purse, but instead the one trying to retrieve it?" "Yes, Your Honor," stated the newsstand clerk. The judge looked around and addressed my mother: "Will you please approach the bench?" My mother walked up to the judge and I sensed that she was embarrassed.

The judge told my mother that by not taking me home that evening, she had helped introduce me into the criminal world of juvenile delinquency. I was dismissed from the courtroom and sent home. But instead of going home, I went to hang out at the clubhouse with the gang members. I started getting high, going to parties, and messing around with girls much older than I was.

CHAPTER 5

Higher Education

In the seventh grade, I got very angry with my music teachers because they wouldn't recommend me for the Music and Arts High School, saying that I wasn't qualified. I thought that they were just prejudiced until I found out that my friend George Gentile was recommended. George was a great trumpet player and very dedicated. I managed to finish the eighth grade and decided to go on to De Witt Clinton High School, one of the best sports-oriented schools in the nation.

My priorities were shifted more toward the party lifestyle rather than school and sports, and it eventually caught up to me. My freshman year would be my last year attending high school. The following summer I played saxophone with a Latin band that included my friend George Gentile. The band lasted for only the summer, and then all the other members decided to move on with their careers. I couldn't go back to school, so I decided to try and work for a living. I bagged groceries with my cousin Kiro for a few weeks, but at the rate that I was going, it would have taken me three years before I could afford my own apartment.

Brother Lew

Next, I decided to try my hand at selling drugs. I got forty dollars together and bought a bundle from a guy named Freddie the Freeloader, the local pusher. The first day that I was out on Elton Avenue trying to sell heroin, I got robbed. I should've known right then that dealing wasn't for me. Two older junkies wanted to buy some drugs, so I went into a building with them. Before I knew it, they had a knife to my throat and took my drugs.

A week didn't go by before I went back to Freddie to buy more stuff to try again. This time, I hid the drugs in mailboxes, under stairs, in garbage bags, and in cigarette boxes, but never on my person just in case. I never made a profit selling drugs because I was a user.

I used to help guys like Ralph Mercado and Federico Pagani pass out flyers for their Latin dance parties because I could get free tickets to party with the ladies. Dancing became my pastime because that was the one thing that I was good at. Most females that walked on a dance floor would do so with an expectation that they would find good dance partners.

I would stay at the clubs dancing for hours. In the late sixties, more and more black folks were getting into Latin music just as Latin folks were getting into R&B.

I met a beautiful young black woman on a Latin moonlight cruise ship. The ship sailed upstate on the Hudson River while thousands of people listened and danced to the beat of Latin music.

I found out that my date was a little different from the girls from our neighborhood. She was very refined and had probably attended some type of high-class finishing school for girls. She wanted to hang out with me and learn about my culture. She invited me to go with her to a cotillion, which in Spanish is called a *quincenera*.

The cotillion was definitely a high-class shindig, and I felt a little out of place. I did appreciate learning a little about high-class black folks, but I didn't appreciate the fact that they thrived on putting down the lower class, especially their own race. It reminded me of the house slaves versus field slaves mentality. I told my friend that if she wanted to date me that we would have to go on neutral ground. I wouldn't want to go out to Long Island, and she wouldn't have to come to the Bronx.

We decided to meet in Manhattan at the Cheetah. The Cheetah was a mixed club that featured Latin bands on certain nights of the week. I showed her how to dance to Latin music, and she appreciated it. That same night, her brother came to pick her up. He told me that he didn't think I was an appropriate date for his sister.

The news had just come in all over the airwaves about Martin Luther King getting shot and people rioting in Watts, Chicago, and other cities. My date left with her brother, and I stayed behind at the club until they closed. It would be the last time that I would see her or her brother. All the clubs in Manhattan seemed to be closing early due to the Martin Luther King news. It seemed as though thousands of people were pouring out into the streets at the same time.

Some people were upset because they were told to leave earlier than the normal closing time, but the police were trying to avoid a riot before it started. The NYPD was never so wrong—it was a miscalculation that resulted in thousands of intoxicated people being shoved into the streets at the same time. It looked like a New Year's Eve gathering at Times Square. The next scene was unforgettable. One drunk man threw a bottle through a glass store window, and all hell broke loose. People everywhere were breaking glass and vandalizing stores. Many policemen on horseback were trying to steer the crowds toward the subway stations to get them

Brother Lew

off the crowded streets. I hurried my way up to the subway station to get out of Manhattan as fast as I could. The last person I wanted to see on a night like this was an angry policeman. The looting of the stores reminded me of the New York City blackout of 1965. Now it was happening again, but without the blackout. I thanked God for letting me make it home safely.

CHAPTER 6

Rikers Island

My mother had a new man in her life, but I avoided her and started hanging out more in my grandmother's neighborhood. I was living the Vida Loca with no job, no responsibility, and no dependents. One night when I was with some of my friends, we happened to borrow another friend's car, but we didn't tell him that we borrowed it. He reported it stolen, and we got busted in it.

My friend Tony and I were taken to the police station, and I was taken back to juvenile detention. The judge told me that if I stepped in his courtroom once again, he would send me upstate for eighteen months. The court bailiff was pretty cool, and he whispered to me on the way out, "Hey, man, he ain't kidding. I've seen him do it," and I said, "Don't worry, man, you won't see me in this courtroom ever again."

I had to report to Mr. Medina, my probation officer, and he had me move back into my mother's house. I wasn't there long before I started hustling and getting high again. Within a few months, I was a full-blown dope fiend, hustling in the streets every day for a fix.

One night I met a young black woman named Mary who was

looking for some drugs. I helped her get drugs, and she invited me to her house. I went with her that night, and then lived with her for a month. We partied every day and went hustling at night. She used to get doctors to give her prescriptions for pills, and then would sell them on the streets. It was a lucrative business for her because she would convince ten to fifteen doctors a month to write prescriptions for her. She had to make sure that she didn't go back to the same doctor before the thirty days were up.

A month later as I left her house in search of a hustle for the day, I noticed a police cruiser approaching me. There were three cops in the cruiser—two veterans and a rookie. The cops stopped me, searched me, and took me to jail. It was that fast and easy because they were trying to teach the rookie that in the Bronx they were the kings of the street and we were the animals.

I was grateful that they didn't charge me with a murder or something more severe. They did, however, charge me with a drug instrument. Supposedly, a bottle cap that was found next to me could've been used as a drug instrument. I couldn't believe that I was a victim of this system. I tried to plead with them to let me go, but they told me I would have to cop out to the charge first and then they'd let me go home. I was sick and in need of a shot of heroin, so I agreed to plead out so they would let me go free.

While we were in the courtroom, the judge decided that I was in no condition to go home, so he sent me to Rikers Island for two weeks.

I wanted out right then. My nose was dripping, my bones were aching, my mind was foggy, and I couldn't get a fix. They took me back to the holding cell where I waited another three hours until the bus for Rikers Island came. The bus finally arrived, and we all had to wait to get our seating positions for the ride. I was very weak and delirious, and had thrown up in the toilet about four times in six hours.

I was trying to figure out how I got caught up in this situation and how I could possibly get out of it, but the thought quickly shattered when the guard came in to get us. The guards had chainlocked two men to a pair of handcuffs and leg chains. If one man would try to escape, the other was sure to slow him down.

The bus to Rikers Island had to stop at different checkpoints before it finally got to its destination. When we arrived at the receiving room, we had to get out and wait to get the handcuffs off, the fingerprints on, the mug shots out, the bug spray in, the strip search through, and then the famous hard bologna sandwich. An average of fifty guys came in to Rikers Island every hour from various courts in the New York City area that evening. All new arrivals went through the same routine until they would reach their cellblocks.

It wasn't until about five o'clock the next morning that we got in to see the nurse. She gave everyone two aspirins and told us to move on. After submitting to quick physicals and signing medical consent forms, we were marched into the infamous Rikers Island tunnel that houses all the cellblocks.

The first gigantic steel door of cellblock number two separated five hundred convicts from the peaceful outside corridor. When the steel vault cellblock door was opened, the noise was deafening. It almost sounded like being in the middle of a stadium concert.

I got up to my jail cell on the third-floor tier of the cellblock. I put my stuff on the bunk, lay down, and slept for hours. It had been a few days since I had taken a bath, but most of my time was spent in the cell sleeping, sweating, and throwing up. I had the shakes, the chills, the smells, and the ills, but the nurse wouldn't give me any pills.

The prisoners from the nearby cells would sometimes call the guards when they thought I was hurting myself by banging my head on the cell walls. I did it mainly to keep the real pain from hurting me. I never would have thought that kicking a heroin habit would be this rough.

My two weeks at Rikers Island were up, and now I had to face the judge, but not before having two helpings of powdered eggs and some coffee that tasted like mud. Six hours later, I got to see the judge. My legal aid lawyer briefly explained to the judge that I was framed by the police, and that the only evidence that they had was a bottle cap without a trace of residue. He also brought up the fact that I didn't give the police permission to search me.

The judge asked the rookie policeman his reason for stopping me, and the officer told the judge that he believed that I was carrying drugs.

The judge told the cop that he didn't have probable cause to search me, so I was let go. I was happy to get out of Rikers Island, but little did I know that my probation officer was in court, ready to take me into custody.

CHAPTER 7

Reform School

I could not believe what was happening to me after my release from Rikers Island. Mr. Medina, my probation officer, was taking me back to Spofford Juvenile Detention Center to prepare me to go to an upstate reform school. I was in Spofford for about two weeks before I boarded the bus for the New Hampton State Training School near Middletown, New York.

New Hampton didn't turn out to be as bad as I had thought it would be. I got a chance to go to school, play sports, and chop down trees. Every once in a while, my mother or my friend Lantys would come up to see me, which would cheer me up for awhile. My mother had just given birth to a new baby boy, and she brought him up to see me. My new baby brother was small and round and looked as if he was going to be a big baby. My mother looked happier than I had seen her in a long time. I guess this marriage was working out for her—no more beatings, no lying, no cursing, no yelling, no fighting, and no more "me" around to give her headaches.

I was glad for my mother—she deserved some happiness in her life. I was a little sad when my mother left the visiting room, but I had to get back to my life in reform school. I was in New Hampton during the time of the Woodstock Festival, only about twenty-five miles from the actual location. I went to the parole board on the seventh month of my sentence and I was given a month and a visit, which meant that I could go home for a week.

I was given a chance to go and stay at my mother's house for one week in the month of April in 1970. While visiting my old neighborhood, I found out that Mary, the girl I had stayed with for a month before I was arrested, was now pregnant and about to give birth to our child. The unexpected news was shocking at first—it was a strange feeling for me to accept the idea that I was about to become a father.

I got together with Mary upon my release, and we tried to make it as a family for baby Angelique's sake. It was hard trying to find a job at the age of seventeen without a high school diploma. My daughter and my baby brother were only a few months apart in age. Time went by and I got deeper into drugs, so deep that I overdosed on heroin twice and almost lost my life both times—once while on a rooftop, and the other time in the street.

CHAPTER 8

Revolving Door

Mary and I moved out of the Bronx and into Manhattan. We had tried a few places downtown before she called the cops on me. Mary was jealous because the girls in our building would come to our apartment looking for drugs. I had started listening to more rebellious types of political music such as Marvin Gaye, Last Poets, Curtis Mayfield, Bob Dylan, Jim Croche, and John Lennon. It wasn't long before Mary and I had split up and I just continued to get into trouble on my own.

One day while I was coming out of a drug dealer's house, I flagged down a cab, got in, and headed for home. A few minutes into the ride, I panicked because I thought I left my wallet at the dealer's house, so I asked the driver to take me back. The driver refused to go back, so I got mad and started shouting at him. The cab driver panicked, jumped out of the cab, and flagged down an oncoming police car.

When I saw what was happening, I jumped out of the cab and ran down the street with the policeman in pursuit. Halfway down the block, the police officer tried to block my path with his car, but I just ran around it. The policeman got out of the car, aimed, and shot at me six times. I was shocked and scared, but I just kept on running until I turned the corner on Intervale Avenue. I quickly crossed the street and ran up to the roof of a building, taking only a second to catch my breath and to check out my surroundings. I looked down and saw that about ten patrol cars were in the street and policemen were now searching the hallways. I immediately jumped over three consecutive rooftops and came down the stairs two blocks away from the scene.

As I landed on the first-floor steps, I saw a homeless person passed out under the stairway, so I decided to take his long, dirty overcoat and his winter hat. I put the coat on and pulled the hat over my face and walked into the street with a limp just in case a police car came by. It so happened that my wallet was found in the back seat of the same cab later on that evening and it was turned over to the Detectives' Bureau. They charged me with robbery, but I eventually copped out to a simple assault and got ninety days at Rikers Island.

CHAPTER 9

Bangin'

While at Rikers Island, I met Tito, who was the Puerto Rican comedian in our cellblock. We became good friends in the joint. We would talk for hours about how we were going to stop using drugs and start making money. We got out a few days from each other and met at a doctor's office. From that the day on, Tito and I were inseparable. We started selling pills, marijuana, and acid together. We both joined a gang called the Ghetto Brothers. They had more than thirty different chapters in New York City. We belonged to the Claremont chapter. Karate Pete was the president of that chapter. I started out providing the music, the weed, and the acid for the chapter, and after a while I became the minister of peace. My job was to make and keep the peace with other gangs.

One day, I left Tito for a few hours to go home, take a shower, and get dressed. My sister Isabel, Tito, and I were going to go out to celebrate my birthday. I picked up my sister, took a cab, and headed out for Claremont, but when we arrived there, we didn't find Tito. Some of our friends told us that he was taken to the hospital.

We heard different rumors, and none of them sounded good, so we decided to go to the hospital and check it out for ourselves. My sister and I took another cab and went to the hospital, but when we got there, it was already too late. Tito had been pronounced dead on arrival. I was in total shock. I couldn't believe that my best friend was dead. I cried, my sister cried, his mother and sisters cried. We all felt the hurt and pain in that hospital room that day.

All I wanted was revenge for my homeboy's murder, but I couldn't do anything because I was the minister of peace. At that moment, I didn't care about the position or the gang. I just wanted my friend back, which I knew was impossible. His mother managed to calm me down, and I realized that his entire family was feeling my pain.

All the gangs in the city called a truce to pay respect at Tito's funeral. He had been stabbed to death by three guys who were drunk. They weren't in a gang themselves, but they were brothers. No one will ever know the reason for Tito's death, even though all three brothers went to jail under a protection warrant. They had to watch their backs in prison because they killed a gang member from a pretty well-known gang.

The word was out from the Black Spades, the Black Pearls, the Savage Nomads, the Brothers and Sisters, the ChingaLings, and others that there would be a truce and peace for a while.

Tito's death had gotten me closer to his sister Edna. A few months later, I started to date her. Edna and I got so serious that I started making plans to leave the gang scene altogether and get married. I was waiting for Edna to graduate from high school so that we could get married, but little did I know that there was a traitor amongst us who had planned to set me up and take over my territory.

People had warned me about Little T, but I didn't want to believe

Bangin

the warnings. He set me up, and I was arrested and sent to jail for ten months. Edna's mother got wind of what was going on, and she sent her daughter away from the neighborhood.

CHAPTER 10

Napanoch State Prison

Rikers Island was overcrowded, so the Department of Corrections allowed inmates with over six months to go to a state prison to do their time. I was sent to Napanoch State Prison in Ellensville, New York. Napanoch had some of the largest prison walls in the system. They were over fifty feet tall with walkways for the guards to travel back and forth across the entire perimeter. While at Napanoch, I received ninety days in solitary confinement for fighting.

In the middle of a basketball game, I was sucker-punched by a young Muslim guy from Brooklyn who didn't like Hispanics. When I tried to retaliate, I was restrained and taken to solitary confinement. I quit smoking during my ninety days there, but once I was released, I started up again.

When I got out of the hole, I was approached by some of the guys from the Spanish mob in Napanoch. They wanted me to click up with them.

The Spanish mob controlled a third of the population and most of the armory in Napanoch. Non-Hispanics were considered outsiders.

Brother Lew

The Spanish mob boss's name was Jimmy "Teenager" Villa. Teenager was a nice guy to his friends, but a not-so-nice guy to his enemies.

If he had his way, Teenager would have wasted all of the five-percenters and the Muslims. While doing time at Napanoch, I got my GED and start reading political books by authors such as Mao Tse Tung, Malcolm X, Piri Thomas, Che Guevara, Eldridge Cleaver, Claude Brown, The Black Panther Party, Angela Davis, The Young Lords Party, H. Rapp Brown, and others. I got into the whole Puerto Rican Liberation state of mind while at Napanoch.

CHAPTER 11

Music Was My Refuge

When I got out of Napanoch State Prison, I decided to move uptown to 183rd Street near the Grand Concourse. I loved that neighborhood because it was mixed with Jewish, Irish, Italian, Spanish, and African Americans.

When I first moved to that neighborhood, I dated two Irish girls, one Italian girl, and a few Spanish girls, but none came close to a pretty Indian-looking Puerto Rican nurse that lived across the street from me.

It wasn't long before Norma and I started to cohabitate. She would leave to go to work at the VA hospital, and I would go down to manage my new social club. Norma and I were perfect dance partners so we enjoyed going out dancing. On the weekends that we didn't go out dancing, I would bring my DJ equipment to the club and spin some records for the customers. The club had pool tables, games, and food-vending machines. The percentage that I was receiving every month from the machines would pay for the rent and upkeep of the place, but to make a profit, I had to dabble in other things.

I eventually traded the small club scene and started to produce larger events such as dances and concerts. I worked with various promoters to do gigs in Manhattan and the Bronx, but nobody promoted like Ralph Mercado when it came to dances and concerts. I also helped manage some of the most notorious after-hours clubs in New York City such as the Nest and Pozo's in Spanish Harlem.

I was getting recognized in the music industry for promotions, production, and management in Latin and disco music. I learned very quickly that the music industry was a very shady business. While I was legally promoting dances and concerts, I was also sharing drugs with big-name celebrities, managers, promoters, radio announcers, club owners, and label execs.

Whoever possessed the drugs had the power, and that is why the Cubans and the Colombians were always trying to outdo each other to show who had the most power. I went to Florida to check out some discos, and one night I was awakened at 3 a.m. in a Hialeah hotel room by two DEA agents who were looking for an out-of-towner to harass. I didn't want to become a statistic in Florida, so I left and went back to New York. When I got home a few weeks later, I found out that I was missing thousands of dollars worth of drugs. Norma told me that her brother Pete had stayed at the house for a few days.

I was very angry, and I had told her that I was going to kill Pete because he had stolen my drugs. She said that if I shoot him then she'll lose a brother and a husband at the same time, and she didn't want that. If Norma hadn't stopped me that night, I probably would still be doing time.

Pete called the next day and told Norma that he had some money to give me. When he finally sent the money with his sister one week later, it totaled only two thousand dollars. He told his sister that more money was coming, but I knew better. How did I know? Because I know how a junkie thinks, I know how a junkie talks, I know how a junkie works, and I know how a junkie acts, because I was a junkie myself. I was never so glad that I no longer had any urges to use heroin. I could see now all the changes that a junkie would go through just so that he could support his habit.

There were too many shootouts and too many people dying in those Spanish Harlem after-hour clubs so I decided to start a safe club up in the Bronx. I rented out a gigantic poolroom and converted it into a dance hall and called it The Latin Manor. I would produce big-name events and rent out the halls to other groups that were also producing events. Some of the wildest events were put on by the Jamaican posse up on White Plains and Gunhill Road.

A few months later at one of my events, I was approached by George MaGoo, an ex-con on parole for murder. Before going to prison, George used to own the "The Sit-n-Chat" club in Spanish Harlem, and now, eight years later, he was looking to get back into the business. George wanted me to run the club, play the music, and gather the ladies, and he would supply the male clientele, the drinks, and the drugs.

CHAPTER 12

In Da Mix

A few months later, I left the big club that I had operated on the weekends to concentrate on the smaller twenty-four-hour joint that we called the Casa Latina. We installed vending games, a jukebox, and a bar. The place was strictly for our customers who would buy drinks or drugs. Within a few weeks we had to issue a policy of checking guns at the door. Even though many didn't want to leave their guns, we convinced them that it was for their own protection.

One day one of our runners named Joey sold coke and marijuana to an undercover cop. Ten minutes later, the drug task force broke down the door to our club. Eight of us were arrested. George and I were charged with drugs and gun possession. Twenty-four hours later, George had posted bail for everyone and business returned to normal.

I was getting tired of taking guns away from drunken patrons who thought they were cowboys living in the wild, wild west. One day I got between George and one of his friends named Carino. They were both high and had their guns aimed at each other. I took

Brother Lew

away their guns and separated them. Many people thought that night that I would surely get shot in the process.

CHAPTER 13

Hit List

Who were these gangsters? Didn't they care about anyone or anything except making money and taking out anyone who got in their way? That's not me. That's not what I want to be. I looked around the room and I thought to myself, "Look at these guys. They're all in the same place, and most of them can't stand each other. They're only together because they need each other to make money."

Georgie McGoo, Louie Italiano, Carlito Corvetta, Pedro Luis, Arania, Roman, Rogelio Carino, Papi Boricua, Jimmy "Teenager" Villa, and Cucho Reveron—all distinct personalities. These were all modern-day gangsters who not only sold drugs, but also used drugs, which was their biggest downfall. A drug user and abuser will remain one as long as he is still using drugs.

One night I got a call from George to close down the club because the cops were looking for him for another murder. He was arrested that same night, but within the week he was out on bail of twenty-five thousand dollars. We knew that trouble was coming because George had killed a rival mobster. It wasn't long before

Kenny Kaiser, Cucho Reveron, and various Cuban imports from Miami were on the lookout for George. Both rival gangs finally shot it out at Frankie Santana's club on Southern Boulevard in the Bronx.

When the dust cleared, a few people were down. George was shot up pretty bad, and one of Cucho's hitmen from Miami was killed. A big meeting was held in the hospital, and I was called in. George asked me to go to Miami to kill Cucho Reveron because he believed that Cucho wouldn't be expecting a hit from me. I immediately refused and walked out of the meeting. That would be the last time that I would speak to my partner George. What I didn't realize was that because I walked out on George's offer, he was going to put out a contract on me so that there wouldn't be any loose ends.

You see, I was the only one who knew of George's plans to kill Cucho, so I was a threat to him. Two weeks later, Cucho was caught in Miami and transported backed to New York to face other charges. My friend Crazy Ray called to tell me that Carlito Corvette and Roberto had accepted the contract on my life. I met with Ray and we both went out looking for the guys who would be trying to kill me. We finally caught up with and confronted Carlito and Roberto. Even though we had the upper hand, we let them try to make the first move. They both backed down and told us that they weren't going to go through with it.

Ray assured them that if something were to happen to me, he would go looking for them and their families. I believe Ray's words got through to them because they both left town. Two months later, George died on the operating table while the doctors tried to remove a bullet near his heart. After that incident, Ray and I had each other's back and we started dealing with guys from our old neighborhood.

One afternoon a few months later, the cops raided Ray's hideout while I was hanging out there with him. Homicide detectives were looking for Ray for a murder that was committed the summer before in Saint Mary's Park in the Bronx. We were both arrested. Ray was charged with murder, and I was charged with everything else, including possession of a half pound of cocaine, heroin, and marijuana, as well as fourteen weapons.

Ray told the cops that I didn't know anything about the drugs or the guns in the house, but they didn't believe him. The prosecutor wanted to give me fifteen years to life unless we cooperated and gave him the name of our dealer. Ray finally told them that he would cooperate. He plea bargained and received a four-year-to-life sentence. Ray told the prosecutor that George MaGoo was his connection. Little did the prosecutor know that George MaGoo had died a few months before on the operating-room table.

At the sentencing, the judge gave me one year to life and Ray got four years to life. I knew that when I got to Rikers Island, I would have to face Cucho Reveron or his nephew Kenny Kaiser because they were both locked up there. Ray told me that he would talk to them if he saw them first. I was put in the homicide cellblock for a day, and I saw someone that I had met in the street. His name was Armando Colon, and he had done eighteen years in prison for murder. Two years prior to that, he was released on parole and now he was back again for murder. He was accused of ripping off dealers and then killing them. Chills went down my spine when I first heard this, because when I first met him, he had just gotten out on parole and was looking for quantity drugs. I could have easily been his next target, but I thank God for looking out for me even then, when I didn't deserve it.

Armando had done time with both George and Cucho and he

couldn't believe that the rivalry between them had gotten so out of hand.

The very next day I was transferred over to the number five block. I saw Cucho and we talked. He realized that I had nothing to do with George's mess and that I wasn't his enemy. I didn't see Ray again until I got to Sing Sing, which was on the day of the strike. The Department of Corrections went on strike and the governor called in the National Guard to take over the prison.

The National Guard didn't want any inmate problems so they brought in pizza and marijuana to keep them happy. The day the strike was over, the convicts almost had a race riot over a softball game on the yard. A black guy pushed a Spanish guy, and within minutes everyone in the yard had a bat or a homemade knife.

The entire population was locked down for two days while the yard was being searched for weapons. I saw Rogelio Carino and Crazy Ray before I had boarded the bus for Danemora State Prison.

I will never forget the reception that we got when the bus pulled into Danemora.

The lieutenant came into the bus and called out the biggest guy to the front. The inmate was about six feet, four inches tall, with at least 250 pounds of pure muscle on him. They pulled him off the bus and about ten C.O.'s started to hit him with clubs.

The inmate was dragged away, never to be seen again. Once again the Lieutenant came into the bus and said, "Now that we understand each other, I want you to come to the front when your name is called. Put your box on the floor, touching the heel of the man in front of you while you stare at his head. When we hit the stick once, you walk; when we hit it twice, you stop."

That was a chilling experience, but I guess it worked because I didn't hear a sound out of anyone for about two days. More strange stories came out of Danemora, and I was trying to stay out of the way so I didn't become a statistic. I finally qualified for minimum status after I received a sentence reduction. The Supreme Court had reduced my sentence from a one-year-to-life to a one-to-three-year sentence. That was the best news I heard since I had been locked up.

CHAPTER 14

Couldn't Handle It

I was finally paroled one year and one day later. Norma and I got back together and moved into a better neighborhood in the Kingsbridge section of the Bronx. I started working as a salesman for a TV company and also started to publish a TV events guide.

A few months later, I got a call from a guy named Rafael who had done time with me at the prison camp. He was interested in purchasing large quantities of heroin, and since I knew that he was into heroin, I didn't question his motives. I called around and made a contact with an old Puerto Rican friend who was tied into the Italian mob's heroin ring. He met with me to discuss the quantities and prices, and then I introduced him to Rafael.

Within a few days Rafael bought an ounce of heroin and I was given a fee for the referral. Rafael loved the stuff because it was uncut pure China white, which was something he had never seen. Rafael was used to the brown heroin that came in from Mexico and Canada, but never this white stuff.

He immediately arranged to purchase larger amounts of this new China white heroin that had infiltrated New York City. White heroin wasn't new to veteran hustlers from Harlem or the Bronx, because most of the heroin in those neighborhoods came from Thailand or Vietnam. Nicky Barnes, Fred Williams, and Goldfinger were three dealers who sold Asian white heroin in Harlem, Brooklyn, Chicago, and the Bronx. I wouldn't be surprised if all of their shipments came from the same source. A lot of controversy hit home when people found out that some Vietnam veterans who were sent back home in body bags were also carrying heroin shipments. The Armed forces found out about it, but only a few people were ever sent to prison for it. Everyone who knew about it suspected that the CIA was behind it.

Selling to Rafael went on a few more times until September 2, 1980. That's when seventy-five DEA agents arrested me along with seven other guys in one of the biggest drug busts in New York City. It wasn't until that evening that I found out that I was involved in a seventy-five-million-dollar drug bust. The news was on every TV channel and newspaper. The next day it appeared in the New York Post, the Daily News, and the New York Times.

The newspapers made it look as though we knew each other, but the truth was that I had just met all but two of the guys. I heard that a snitch was in the camp. It wasn't until I reached the federal lockup that I realized where the real gangsters were. The feds had terrorists, bank robbers, mafia dons, political prisoners, former leaders of foreign countries, and politicians locked up in their prisons.

Many guys became celebrities because of their federal cases. Among those who crossed my path were the Giacolone Brothers—one was convicted for the Jimmy Hoffa case and the other for racketeering charges in Florida. A guy named Sindona was responsible for a Vatican-owned bank going broke. Others included Carlo the Mob Bomber and Gentleman Jim of the Luftansa robbery and the movie Goodfellas. It was like a "Who's Who" in federal prison. I couldn't believe that I had been released from a life sentence almost a year ago and now I was back in the joint about to do federal plus state time.

I had gotten in trouble again because I didn't focus on my goal to stay out of prison; instead, I tried to go for the quick money and landed back inside again. Norma was five months' pregnant and I had no way to get out of the mess that I had put myself in. The feds sent me out to Oxford, Wisconsin, where I took on a trade. The prison had an associate's degree program with the Fox Valley Technical College in Hotel Restaurant Cookery and in Hotel Restaurant Management. I heard that this was one of the fastest ways to get parole, so I enrolled in the cooking school.

Two years later, I received two associate's degrees from Fox Valley and I went on to get an associate's degree from the University of Wisconsin. I was given an early parole to a halfway house because of my exemplary record in the institution.

I had applied for and received a job only forty-eight hours after I had checked in to the federal halfway house. I was hired as an assistant manager at Roy Rogers Restaurant near Wall Street. Two weeks later, I went home to visit Norma and I realized that she had changed in the last four and one-half years. She looked paler and skinnier than I had ever had seen her before. She finally broke down and told me that she was using cocaine on a daily basis with her brother and sister-in-law. I tried not to let the past get in the way of our future, but she kept sneaking off to use drugs. After three months, I had to put a stop to the situation. I tried to convince her to get help or else I would have to leave the house. I didn't want anything to do with drugs, especially since our son Angel was living in the house with us.

I was on parole and I wanted her to get into a rehab center so that we could continue with our lives. I came home from work one day and found some aluminum paper with cocaine inside. I quickly flushed it and I went to her brother's house to tell her that I was leaving. As I entered the house, I saw her sniffing cocaine through a straw. I told her, "You aren't going to change, so I have to leave until you do." I was hoping that my moving out of our apartment would motivate her to get some help.

Two days later, I came back to see if I could take Angel with me until Norma had finished a rehab program, but Angel wasn't at his grandmother's, and neither was Norma. Further investigation led me to believe that she had moved out of the apartment. It was confirmed an hour later when I called her employer to try and get some information, but I was told that she hadn't been to work and hadn't called. I called everybody but got no response.

Two weeks later, she called to tell me that Angel and her were all right and that she left so she could get some help. She told me not to worry or to try getting in touch with her, and that she would call me when she was ready to come back. She was in Puerto Rico with her brother and sister-in-law, and her mother had also moved there. How was I to know that I never would see Norma alive again?

We spoke on and off for a while, but she was still using and didn't know when she was going to stop. Six months later I got laid off, and decided that I had had it with New York, so I asked my federal parole officer if I could move out of state, so she brought it up for review. A few weeks later, I was approved by the Cleveland area office to move to Ohio for the remainder of my parole.

I moved out of New York and I decided that I wanted to start a new life. I met a friend named Edna who was a close friend of my family and we started dating. After my unemployment ran out, I looked for a job. A few months later, I started to work for Rent-A-Center on the weekdays, and on the weekends I would promote Latin dances in the Cleveland and Lorain areas.

The people were happy to see Latin dance parties come back into the area, but other dance promoters were not so pleased. They had carved out many years of promoting dances and they were not going to let an out-of-towner come in and take over their operations. I sensed rejection in the air when I went out to speak to the various promoters. I was told by many that certain things were done certain ways in these areas, and the reason that many promoters had stopped promoting was that certain artists were not showing up when they were promoted on the dance nights.

I introduced the promoters to performance agreements and riders that would hold up in court in any state of the union. Most of the promoters wanted to shy away from the courts and all their legalities. When one would express reluctance, I would respond that if he didn't want to run his business as a business, then he shouldn't complain when his business goes under.

Many didn't like my attitude, but I wasn't in this business for them to like me—I had to take care of the business the best way that I knew. When the promoters in the areas stopped promoting dances, most of the social clubs took over that function in the community.

Now that I was promoting dances on a larger scale than the regular small social clubs, the clubs had to take a stand. The clubs would wait for me to bring in an out-of-town artist and then would hire a local artist for the same day and not charge for the local dance party. They believed that many more people would go to a free party than a paid party, especially if they had to pay to see the artist perform.

I would pull in a lot of people but not enough to cover all the expenses, the promotion, and the bands. After the same situation happened a few times, I decided to call a meeting with all the local bands in a fifty-mile radius. I told them that I would promote a dance every week in different areas and would use each band at least once per month, and they all agreed. Most of the clubs would hire them only for special occasions even though they were open every day.

This was the ammunition that I needed to get the cooperation of the clubs and promoters. I met with them and explained that I had every Latin group under contract and I would want to work out a round-robin approach with each of them. The round robin would allow everyone to participate once per week in an event with all the others promoting or approving the event. This way, the bands would get work and the clubs would have customers who ordinarily wouldn't go to them. It worked well for a short time, and then I had to pull out for a while.

While I was promoting a Lakeside beach concert, I met a few girls I was trying to recruit to compete for the Miss Latina Pageant contest. Little did I know that one of them would be my future wife. When I met Elena, she was trying to get my attention. But when I finally spoke to her, she thought my cousin was my girlfriend. She was shy but frisky, and I had to tell her that I was going out with someone.

I would see her on and off, and she would always ask me if I had a girlfriend. It didn't matter if I said "yes," because she would always then ask why she never saw her. I told her that one day she'd meet her. Then one day we were promoting a Latin Jam concert at Oakwood Park in Lorain. Hundreds of people were dancing and having a good time. Finally, I saw the opportunity to introduce Edna to Elena. Elena finally realized that I was telling her the truth, that I did have a girlfriend. About six months later, Edna and I split up, and I moved to another section of town.

One Saturday evening, some of my fellow workers at Rent-A-Center were having a going-away party for one of the girls who worked with us, and I decided to invite my friend Elena. The party was at a nice place called Mountain Jacks and Elena seemed to like it. A few months after that, I became the manager at our store for awhile. I enjoyed working with the employees as well as the customers.

Just when everything was going well, I got into an accident at work and I went on disability for about seven months. I was experiencing a lot of pain in my back, and the pain pills that I was taking weren't helping much. I started to drink every night. I had stayed off of drugs for over five years, and now, due to a back injury, I was using again. It scared me because this was exactly how I started using the first time. I remembered that it was the pain from the operation that got me hooked on morphine and then on heroin. All the pain in the world would never get me to go back to the past. Still, I was drinking, smoking, and sniffing coke, and I should have known better.

CHAPTER 15

I Should Have Known Better

Yes, I should have known better, but by this time I was running out of my workman's comp benefits. Rent-A-Center didn't have a management opening in our area, and Elena was pregnant. I made a few trips to New York and Cleveland to try to score some marijuana, but I didn't find any pot. What I did find was some coke.

A few weeks later, as I arrived in Lorain, Ohio, I was set up and arrested by the Lorain County Drug Task Force. Only a few people knew that I was in Lorain at that precise moment, so I knew they had set me up. They had called me up and asked me to meet with them at the Oakwood shopping center, and I went for the meeting. I went into a store and looked around and didn't see them. But when I came out of the store, I was surrounded by a bunch of police officers with their guns drawn. Eddie Young, one of the drug task force officers, had a search warrant for my car and my apartment.

The officers found a few ounces of cocaine. I went to court and the judge gave me a forty-thousand-dollar bail. My friends Edna and Anna Carrion, as well as Elena, helped me get out on bail. They

Brother Lew

took four thousand dollars to my friend Emmett Ross, a bail bondsman in Lorain, and he had me released.

While I was out on bail, I didn't go anywhere. I didn't go outdoors or do anything but wait for my court appearance, but four weeks later the case was postponed. As I walked out of the courtroom, two federal marshals approached me, arrested me, and took me to the Cleveland federal holdover jail. My federal parole officer had concluded that I had violated my parole even though I had not been convicted of the current crime.

It seemed that the prosecutor didn't think that it was wise for me to be on the streets since a gun was found on the premises. "A gun? I don't own a gun," I thought out loud. These people were trying to frame me. Then I remembered about the gun that they were talking about. It was found in a compartment inside of the oven, and belonged to one of my friends who came over to my house drunk one night. Since he was drunk, I took the gun from him and hid it inside the oven. I had forgotten all about it until the day of the bust. My lawyer, Jack Bradley, received a signed affidavit from my friend stating that the gun belonged to him, but I should have known better.

Being in the same room with a gun gave me access to that gun, and that was an immediate cause for parole violation. If I would've remembered that, I wouldn't have gotten out on bail, because that was four thousand dollars wasted. I had only been out on bail for four weeks before the marshals re-arrested me. They started to offer me fifteen years, but I told them that I would fight it all the way. I talked it over with Elena, and on the day of my jury selection, I copped a plea of three to fifteen years in the state prison.

All that I could think of at that time was all the years that I have to do for the state and the feds. I was very angry and very hurt. I was angry at myself, I was angry at the system, I was angry at my family, and I was angry at the father that I never knew. I was angry at my mother for leaving my father and for bringing me to this God-forsaken land. I was angry that I ever experimented with drugs. I was angry for being poor, and I was angry for being Puerto Rican. I was angry.

Silent anger and silent fear—these are the same symptoms that can lead one to depression, oppression, and suicide. Hey, wait a minute—I'm not trying to go out like that. I better change this attitude really quick.

CHAPTER 16

Institutionalized?

I went to the joint with silent anger. My first six months in the joint were rough because I was angry and didn't care who I would take it out on. The judge had given me permission to marry Elena. But even though we both signed a marriage certificate and took a blood test, we passed the thirty-day expiration time limit. I couldn't get any visits for the first thirty days, and by then it was already seven days into our countdown. We both agreed that if it was God's will that it would happen.

One day while I was at Orient Correctional Institution, a guy from Cincinnati was blocking my way as I was coming out of the bathroom. I told him to move, but he hesitated and looked back at his buddies. He laughed, but as he was turning back to me saying the words, "Who's gonna," Bam! I struck him with one punch on the right side of the jaw, and he went down and out cold.

As I stepped over his body, I said, "Anybody else wanna get in my way?" They looked at me as though they wanted to jump me, but they weren't sure if I was able to take them all on, and then again they wouldn't have wanted to go out like their buddy did.

They didn't think twice—they just picked him up from the floor and left. At that precise moment, some of the Cleveland guys were coming into the bathroom.

One of them said "Yo' man, I keep telling you about these crazy Puerto Ricans. You Cincinnati boys don't have a clue until ya'll get cut up with a switch blade." They were all laughing at the Cincinnati crew. One guy asked me, "Yo' man, you did that?" and I replied, "No man, he did it to himself." He said, "Yo' man, I liked that one. Where you from, man, the west side?" I said, "No, I'm from New York, but I moved to Lorain when I came out on parole from the federal joint."

Once I had mentioned that I was from New York and had done time, I automatically qualified to hang out with the Cleveland crew. The guys from Cincinnati were cool after that day, and the guy that I had knocked out couldn't remember what had happened to him because he was high on pills. Orient Correctional Institution wasn't the toughest prison that I had been in, but it sure was the weirdest. There would be late night parties in the dormitories. The lights and the music were turned on as the drag queens would start dancing in the isles. The wine makers would stash their wine in the ceilings for fermentation purposes and the party would get live.

There were about twenty showers, twenty toilets, and two TV rooms for three hundred convicts in building seven and the same for building eight. I wanted to transfer over to unit six because it wasn't as wild as unit seven. In Orient, most cons kept an eye out for their lockers because they were apt to be involved in a daytime burglary, especially on the day they would go to the commissary.

I got involved in the daily mix of the institution—the hustling, dealing, lying, and conniving ways of survival in prison. It was just another day and another way of life until your number came up.

Institutionalized?

Inmate stores charged needy inmates a two-for-one payback of any credited items.

Inmate-run stores carried grocery items, cigarettes, money, wine, drugs, new prison dress clothes, or even steak sandwiches from the kitchen. I ran a store for a while until I got locked up for suspicion of drug trafficking. After I was released from solitary investigative lockup, I was moved to Dorm Building number six.

CHAPTER 17

The Truth Will Set You Free

On August 16, 1988, I was playing softball, and as I slid into home plate, I felt a sharp pain shoot up through my arm as my wrist snapped back.

I was sent to the nurse, and she gave me a bottle of Motrin. After about half an hour and eight Motrins later, I started to feel hot and drowsy. The 4 p.m. count was underway and we couldn't interrupt it even if we had an emergency. I put on my earphones and lay down on the bed to listen to some music while the pills took effect.

On the radio, some guy was talking to teenagers about some satanic stuff, and then he said, "You can't go another day without Jesus, because only he can save you. Tomorrow wasn't promised to you. If you died tonight, would you go to hell?" That's when I said, "Okay, you're history. I don't want to listen to this," but as I tried to stretch out to reach the radio at the foot of the bed, I felt a sharp pain in my back that didn't allow me to move.

I was just frozen there for a few minutes, and then suddenly I felt sick again and I called for the guard. I was sent to the nurse, and she quickly gave me a thermometer to see if I had a fever. The reading topped 110 degrees, and she thought that I had put the thermometer in hot water.

It wasn't until I complained of being cold that she realized that something was very wrong. She called the doctor, gave me a blanket, and started to prepare me for an EKG. I started to feel faint on and off, and I felt as if I wasn't going to wake up again. Then I lost consciousness. I remember calling out to God and asking him for forgiveness, asking for another chance, and asking him not to let me die.

Even though everything was pitch black, I knew that someone was talking to me. The voice didn't sound like a dream when it said, "I've given you plenty of chances but you didn't take them. You took only your own." Everything was silently dark, and it seemed as though I was floating toward a big screen in the ceiling. I started seeing things that had happened to me in the past.

I saw myself taking some guns away from two guys who were about to kill each other. I saw a police officer shooting at me as I was trying to run from him. I saw myself almost dying from heroin overdoses two different times. I saw two guys who were looking to kill me, and then I saw a voodoo priestess putting a curse on me.

I woke up from my comatose state in a sweat. The nurse told me that my kidneys had shut down and I went into a coma. I was in Ohio State University hospital in Columbus, Ohio, and was handcuffed to a hospital bed. I heard snoring all around me, so I knew that other people were in the same room. I didn't want to go back to sleep for fear of falling back into a coma.

As I strained to hear the message coming from the radio in the hall, it started to sound very familiar. Then it hit me—it was that guy again. At first I thought that I was back in the dormitory. I adjusted my ears to hear it louder and clearer. All of a sudden it got louder and I heard exactly what was being said.

It was the same voice that I had heard that afternoon, and I called out to the nurse to ask her about that man on the radio. I told her that I had heard that message that same afternoon and now I'm hearing him again. "Am I going crazy?" "No," she said. "That's Bob Larson, and he has a Christian radio program that comes on everyday at 4 p.m. and at midnight. He usually talks to young people, but maybe today he was talking to you."

What I just heard the nurse say had made me uncomfortable because I almost believed it. I wasn't trying to go back to sleep, so I stayed up and listened to the program. This Larson guy made a lot of sense and he quoted scriptures from the Bible. I didn't know that people would take the Bible so seriously that they would invest time in reading it unless they were going into the priesthood. The few times that I went to Catholic church, we relied on the word of the priest who was reading to us from the Bible, but he would never encourage us to read it for ourselves.

At that very moment, Bob Larson said, "Don't believe me—read it for yourself. The Bible plainly teaches that if you are not saved, you won't go to heaven, so where would you go? Romans 10:10 says that if you call upon the name of the Lord, you will be saved." For the first time in my life, something was happening that didn't involve using drugs. I wanted to call upon the Lord, but I hesitated. I didn't want people to think that I was stupid, even though that kind of thinking has probably cost many people their salvation.

Then Bob Larson said, "Remember that tomorrow isn't promised to any of us; we all can die tonight." I was now seriously contemplating giving myself up to the Lord, but I waited to see if anyone else was going to stop me. Then a lady came by and said, "He's right, you know. Tomorrow isn't promised to anybody."

I don't know if that lady was serious or not, but that's all it took for me to give in. I wasn't waiting any longer. I said, "Lord, I prayed earlier to you to give me another chance, and even though I didn't think that you would do it, you did. I know now that it was you all the time that got in the way of all those bullets, and those times that I was left for dead. I now know, Lord, that it was you all along. It was you, Lord, who took my place and died so I could be free. Help me be a better person and help me get to know more of you. Thank you, Lord, for this second chance."

CHAPTER 18

Parole Anyone?

That was August 16, 1988, and even though I have gone through the valley of the shadow of death, I fear no evil, and I will not regret what my God has done for me. I took on a different outlook on life that day, especially since my life was not really mine any more. God gave me a second chance. He paid for my life so now I will live for him.

God gave me a brand new life to work with, a brand new heart to use, and a brand new body to keep clean from all the mess. Yes, not only did I feel new, but I also looked new.

I remembered that one guy had asked me if I had gotten a parole because of the change in me. In all reality, I didn't get a parole, but I did get a pardon from God for all my past sins. I started to search out Christian teachings on TV, on radio, in books, and in magazines.

I realized that I was an ambassador for Christ, a prince in a royal priesthood, and a servant for the Lord. One day I was trying to pray when a disturbance from a nearby radio kept interrupting my time with God.

Brother Lew

The radio was blasting curse words from a rap tape, and that's when I started to ask God to get rid of all those profane lyrics from those horrible songs.

The Lord kept depositing various scriptures in my spirit that confirmed what I believed that God wanted me to do. I started to write biblical lyrics to new songs in a rap format. It even sounded crazy to me, but I believed that God was trying to make a point. The more I prayed and meditated, the more wisdom that God showed me. I knew that the lyrics that God was giving me would change the lives of young people all over the state.

I started Bible studies in Orient Correctional at one of the side rooms that we used for quiet time in building six. I went to college, worked part-time, and waited to go to the parole board. Now that I was serving God, he would send me home on parole so that I could do his work out in the street and not in this prison. I went to the parole board ready for a release date, but they gave me two more years.

That night I had a long talk with God, and I did all of the talking. It wasn't until I started to meditate on God's word that I started to get answers. I believed wholeheartedly that God wanted to release me, but that I wasn't ready to be released, so I started to get ready for the next time that God would want me to go. Our Bible study group had reached eight guys, and that was great. But no sooner had that happened that I was transferred across the street to Pickaway Correctional, an institution that receives prisoners who are preparing to go home. At Pickaway I worked as the associate warden's runner. I got baptized out in the yard and started to write a lot of songs. Our Bible study group at Pickaway had about twenty-five saints. The Lord kept using me to plant seeds in those who came to the institution for only a few days at a time.

I enrolled into a drug rehab unit to learn about drugs and alcohol and to try and get a transfer to Grafton, a facility that was closer to my family. The time had finally come, and I was given the transfer to Grafton. At Grafton, I saw some of the guys who were with me at prior institutions. I got together with groups of men that would meet for Bible studies and church services.

At Grafton I started to work in the kitchen, take college courses at night, and go into the music room to develop some of my rap songs. I entered a rap contest at the prison and won third place. First place was won by a secular rapper, and second place was won by another Christian rapper. All the glory went to the Lord that day.

I had already gone back to the parole board. They told me to do two more years and then I was to get paroled to my federal warrant. On December 20, 1991, I was paroled to the federal government to answer seven years on a parole violation warrant. The federal marshals came to pick me up and I was transported to Milan, Michigan, then to Oklahoma, only to be sent back to Lewisburg and then to my destination, Mackeon, Pennsylvania.

Mackeon was a fairly new medium-security facility that offered very few opportunities for advancement. I thanked God for the increasing numbers of laborers who were serving him within the prison systems. I saw it start at Orient with eight guys; Pickaway, twenty-five; Grafton, seventy-five; Painsville, eighteen; Milan, one hundred; and Mckeon, one hundred twenty-five. These numbers represented the guys in the joint who had accepted the Lord and were serving the Lord in Bible studies.

Mckeon was special because it had a huge Spanish population serving the Lord, and the institution had services in Spanish as well as English. Some of the Colombian brothers at Mckeon directed the services. I knew that I had to physically show up at the federal parole board hearing even though I already knew that I had seven years coming. The day that I went to the parole board, I met a lawyer from Pittsburgh who came up to handle my case. I didn't know the man or had ever seen him before that day, but if he was going to defend me in front of the parole board, why not? What did I have to lose?

The next half an hour proved to be a very critical point in my life. I was trying to keep calm and hope that I wouldn't get too upset when the parole board would tell me to my face that I had to do seven more years. It was bad enough to know I'd have to do the time, but they wouldn't have to humiliate me by reminding me.

I guess after awhile it didn't matter because I was ready for some humility anyway. Being turned down twice at the parole board and not knowing how much more time that I had to serve was one thing, but now, four and a half years later, I knew I wouldn't do more than seven more years. That made it much easier to handle. I prayed to the Lord to let him know that I was prepared to do whatever time he thought was proper for me, including the full seven years.

The lawyer came out of the hearing room and asked me to come in. I took a seat as a member of the parole board said, "Mr. Acosta, your lawyer has pointed out to us that you were released back to the State of Ohio to resume trial, but after trial the marshals never went back to take custody until now. That was four years and nine months ago. Since then, you have been in custody, and we have to allow that time to offset the full amount of time that you are supposed to serve. Do you have any questions?" I asked, "Do you mean that the marshals made a mistake and I can go home?" She said, "You will be paroled at the fifth year of your incarceration, which will be within the next ninety days." I said, "Thank you," and walked out. I tried to keep my composure, but I was just too excited. I must have thanked that lawyer fifteen times before I went back to my building. I thanked God also because he knew exactly what I needed, and he supplied. He sent a lawyer unknown to me to get me out of the federal prison system. I called Elena that night, and we talked about our marriage plans. Some of the guys that knew me from the joint wanted to keep in touch with me when they got out since they knew that I was leaving soon.

One of them worked for the Italian mob in Chicago, and the other worked for the Cuban mob in New York and Miami. They both gave me their numbers before I left so that I could keep in touch with them if I needed anything. June 20th came, and I walked out of McKeon prison a free man. Elena was waiting for me, and we headed out of town for the county administration building to get a marriage certificate and finally get married.

CHAPTER 19

Free at Last

There's something special about a McDonald's cheeseburger that tastes a hundred percent better when you haven't had one for more than five years. There's also something special when you get to sleep in your own bed after so long. And there is something even more special about being in your own bed with a woman who is your wife after being alone for so long.

Special vows for special people. I vowed to try and go back into the prisons as a minister, an instructor, or as a facilitator, but not as a prisoner. My life now belonged to God. He made sure that I did not come out before he knew I was mature enough to not make the same mistakes that I had done in the past.

I had to report to state and federal parole officers in two different counties, so I had to deal with two separate personalities and twice as many responsibilities as someone with only one parole officer. From the first day that I went to see my state parole officer, I knew that I was in for a challenge. He wasn't there on time for our appointment, and every parolee in the waiting area had a horror story about him sending back ninety percent of his parolees.

I didn't have time for those negative vibes, so I convinced myself that I was going to be on his ten-percent list. He showed up three hours later, and was glad that I was still waiting for him. I let him know that I was serious about following the parole policies to the letter. He told me that when some guys come in, if he's not there, they leave. They don't realize that their priority is not anything in the free world, but their parole. If they don't satisfy their parole officer, they get put back in.

In my case, he was going to give me some slack because he knew that I had two parole officers to satisfy and had to look for a job and enroll in a drug treatment program.

He told me that he wanted me to go to the Lorain County Alcohol and Drug Abuse Services program and get an assessment so that I could start their intensive outpatient program. I explained to my parole officer that I was already going to a Christian-based program called Drug Free Through Christ, and that eventually I would be facilitating that program since I had being doing it in the prison system.

His response to me was to get the assessment first and then whatever I worked out with them and the federal parole officer was okay by him. After a few hours, the assessor realized that not only had I not used drugs or alcohol for the previous five years, but was totally committed to do a Christian-based program with a better success rate than any regular secular program.

I started to do outreach with the Drug Free Through Christ program ministry, headed by Bishop Hannibal and Minister Freddie Garcia. Freddie Garcia was one of the ministers who used to visit the prisons to bring in the Word of God. I met Freddie while I was in Grafton and kept in touch with him after I got out.

I remember that in our first outdoor outreach, I was asked to give

Free at Last

a short testimony before a tent full of people. After I had finished, Bishop Hannibal introduced the evening's speaker, Bishop T. D. Jakes. I had never heard of Bishop Jakes before that evening, but would never forget him after listening to the powerful message he brought that night.

I started to visit churches and give my testimony of what the Lord had done in my life. I didn't get a job right away because I wanted to finish my college education and get my degree.

I applied for and received two student loans to finish my degree. I went to Ashland University to try and get two degrees for the price of one. One of the degrees was in business and the other was in religion.

I needed money to get the outreach ministry started, so Elena and I signed for a loan. I recorded ten outreach songs in a hip-hop format. Even though I was doing outreaches, I was giving out most of the tapes to the kids who answered the altar calls. My wife told me that I would never make the money back giving away the tapes for free. I knew that she was right, but I couldn't deny a kid a tape just because he didn't have five dollars. I had an idea, and spoke to Elena about it. I showed her a newspaper called the Love Express from New York City. If I did the Cleveland edition of the Love Express, it would help sponsor the ministry as well as help us financially until I finished school.

The newspaper was coming about very slowly. The publisher kept telling me that it would take time, but I was impatient to see its fruits. The newspaper carried some very powerful testimonies that were borrowed from other Christian publications. To help supplement the publicity of the newspaper and the ministry, I bought time on Christian radio. I was going to school, doing the newspaper, selling ads, and doing outreaches. It wasn't long before I realized that I was getting burned out. I soon found out that Christians don't all believe the same, act the same, or walk the same. That to me was a reality shock, because in the joint I would always know immediately who was my friend and who was my enemy. Out here, people who I thought would have their integrity in check often screwed me up. I had to stop publishing the newspaper, and six months later I had to stop doing the radio programs.

To make matters worse, I had gone to the Lorain County bank a few times to make my loan payments, but their tellers couldn't take my money because my account number would not come up on the computer. Finally one of the adjusters told me that my loan had been charged off. I didn't comprehend what charged off meant until they explained it to me. My problem with the bank was that they did not take my money when it was due, and now I was charged off. That meant that our credit, Elena's and mine, would be ruined.

Elena had had good credit for more than fifteen years, and now that was over. I went back and forth a few times to the bank to speak to the loan adjusters, but no one would accept responsibility for the mistake. I wanted a letter from the bank stating that it was their fault that this had happened so that I could clear it up with the credit bureaus, but I didn't get anywhere.

I had graduated from Ashland University with dual degreed in Business and Religion. I took on a full-time job at WTOF and WHLO in Akron. It had cost me over three hundred dollars a month to use my car, but their expense check covered only one hundred dollars per month. Things didn't work out as I expected, and I had to leave that job.

I tried promoting other ministries as well as rap and choir groups. I also did gigs and tours with people like the Dynamic Twins, E-Roc, Eric Champion, and others. One night at the end of a concert in Detroit, I was in a restaurant with the Dynamic Twins, E-Roc, Minister George Fitzgerald, Scott Ross, and Charles Wolfork, who was singing backup for us that day. The Lord revealed to me that he wanted me to quit the group and go into prayer. I told Charles Wolfork that I would help him promote his group, but that I had to go into prayer about my own situation.

CHAPTER 20

Seek Ye First

I had to look for a new job because of my family and my bills. I got into prayer, and the doors to the juvenile detention centers were opened to go and minister the Word of God. I gave testimony, preached, and used hip-hop music as a way to reach the mass population. The altar calls were full of young people ready to give their lives to the Lord. I started going into different places with different ministries, and the blessings were tremendous.

I got myself a different job recruiting businesses for temporary agencies. In 1995, I started the Radical Fanatics, the second leg of the rap ministry that was going to continue the outreach work. I became the Sunday youth minister at the Stepping Stone Juvenile resident home, and later on I also took over the position to minister to the females and the runaways whenever they came out to the services. The staff members that participated also enjoyed the services.

The Radical Fanatics were getting very well known in the region, so we started to do outreach in other cities and states. We recorded an album and a video. Just before our video was going to be shown nationally, my partner in the group decided that he was going to go solo. I had assumed the fourteen-thousand-dollar debt that was still pending after producing the music, recording the album, making the video, and doing all the promotion for the group. I had to finish my touring commitments alone, and then I went into prayer. I had worked for four temporary employment agencies in various capacities: as a job developer, salesman, manager, and coordinator, and now I was ready for a change.

In August of 1998, I got a call from a supervisor at the county alcohol and drug abuse agency who wanted to talk to me about a possible job. The supervisor told me that I was recommended as one of the best possible candidates for an available position. I set up an appointment, but I wasn't sure of the position, so I went to investigate. I felt a little relief that it was in prevention, especially since I had been doing a prevention program using arts, music, and employment skills. I prayed over the position, and felt at peace to start working for them, even though it meant that I would have to take a ten-thousand-dollar pay cut.

Since starting that job, I have had the opportunity to help minister to thousands of people who have suffered from at-risk behaviors. We covered all aspects of prevention from stress, conflict, and anger, to decision-making skills that can help individuals make positive choices rather than those that were alcohol or drug related.

I did programs at the jails, prisons, rehab centers, alternative schools, the county mission, and metropolitan housing projects. People who do this type of work get stressed out and burned out very fast, and the agencies usually have a large turnover of workers. I was blessed with the opportunity to see thousands saved as I ministered through my job along with many of my co-workers. I know that very soon the Lord will be opening the doors for fulltime ministry, but until then, I will continue to work in the environment that he has put me in.

God has allowed me to work with various music ministries that have blessed so many over the past ten years. Today I keep in close contact with a few that are still on the battlefield making strides. These people have established ministries, and I ask that we keep them in prayer: Jose David Quintana and Josue Torres, also known as JT the Rapper, both known in the international Christian music scene; Grip, formerly known as DJ Pain; the group Descendantz; J Squad, a Spanish Christian rap duo; Selena Ocasio, a very talented praise and worship singer; Celeste Rivera Cupek, a bilingual Christian contemporary singer; Virgen Camacho, a Spanish Christian contemporary and praise and worship singer; Pete Figueroa, a dynamic urban contemporary Gospel singer; Alex Morris, a Christian salsa singer; Willie and Jessi Velez, a talented urban contemporary Gospel duo; and MouthPiece, my ex-partner in the Radical Fanatics Christian rap group.

In 1998, I worked out a deal to get JT's music out on a compilation album on Rescue Records. In 1999, we were going to partner with Rescue on a Latin division, but they called it off at the last minute. That same year, I started to promote Lampara Music Group. I've been approached by many for various types of opportunities, but I've turned most of them down because they didn't line up with the mission or the vision.

A few more opportunities came my way, but none of them worked out, including a label deal in Hollywood, a distribution deal in South Carolina, and a partnership deal locally. I lost time and money in misguided attempts at furthering the ministry gifts that God had given me. I had allowed myself to get stressed out. I was diagnosed with high blood pressure, diabetes, vocal nodules, and eyesight problems within six months. I knew that this would only be temporary, so I prayed for the Lord to guide my steps. I had been working non-stop trying to catch up to interest-generating loans and credit cards that were used during my unemployment.

In almost ten years since getting out of prison, both my wife and I have paid off more than $74,000 in bills, student loans, bank loans, and credit cards, while paying our regular bills. At times I had even considered filing for bankruptcy, but we didn't because it was our responsibility, so we dealt with the situation regardless of how hard it got. We all deal with stressful situations daily, and I thank God that I put him first in my life. Who knows what type of situation I would have been in if it were not for Jesus in my life?

The morning of September 11, 2001, I stared at the TV in shock as a plane crashed into the World Trade Center in New York City. Nothing in the world seemed as important as the events that were happening before our very eyes. We saw destruction in a way that has never been seen before in our generation. The world stopped and looked at the senseless murders and suicides of those terrorists. Panic had surfaced around the globe. Many felt blessed to be serving a true living God, but many others didn't have a clue about what to think or what to believe. I believe that the events were a wakeup call for the masses. It showed us that the next hour isn't promised to anybody, and we can all die instantly.

In the days that followed September 11th, I found out from my sister that her father had passed away. Her father was my stepfather, the one who used to beat me when I was growing up, the one I used to have nightmares about, the one who made me fight a boy twice my size, and the one I had blamed for my younger sister's death. I felt bad for him and sad at the same time.

I had just come to the realization that not once in my life had I prayed for this man—all those opportunities to pray for people, good or bad, and I had never prayed for this man's soul. Tears came to my eyes as I started to ask God for forgiveness for not remembering him in my prayers. It didn't matter what I personally thought about him—he had helped support me, my mother, and my sister while he was around, and I should be thankful at least for that. I was relieved to find out that my sister prayed for him.

I pray that people don't get so involved in their own emotions that they miss the big picture. We tend to want to put a curse on those that do us wrong instead of praying for God to help them be better people. When we curse others, we only curse ourselves, because we put strain, stress, and anxiety in our paths to sickness. When we pray for others to get help, God will heal them and they can therefore pray for you. The thing that I would most definitely want someone to do for me is to pray for me, because I know that prayer is the communication line between God and man, and God listens to the fervent prayers of a righteous man.

So, if you were to die in the next few minutes, do you know beyond a shadow of a doubt where you would be going? To heaven or to hell? If I were to die in the next few minutes, I would want to have life insurance. The life insurance that I'm talking about is not the type that you buy from an insurance company, but one you are freely given by God. The type of insurance that you buy from a company should actually be called death insurance.

Think about it. Your beneficiaries get paid when you die. So they are insured to get some money when you are dead. But what about you? What type of insurance do you get? The only real life insurance policy that I know of is the eternal life policy with Jesus Christ. When the time comes when I will face Judgment Day before God Almighty, I want to make sure that Jesus is my defense attorney. I know that the devil is going to be my prosecutor, and he's going to tell God about all my sins.

But I know, without a shadow of a doubt, that Jesus will defend me and reassure God the Father that he has already paid for my sins. Jesus will tell God that my place is in heaven because I decided to live for him and not for Satan. I want to ask you the same question: Do you know beyond a shadow of a doubt where you would go today if you died instantly? How about your family members? Do you care enough for them to prevent them from drowning in the lake of fire?

This world is not forever; it is a temporary pit stop. The next world is our eternal destiny, so which will it be? I know that with Christ we have blessed assurance of where we would go. Until our day comes, we have to deal with the daily struggles and the stresses that our environment affords us, but we can make our life much simpler. Read the Word of God and pray so that the Lord will help you deal with all types of situations. When we accept Jesus into our lives, we become new creations, and our old lives are left behind. God wants us to walk in integrity and to be responsible, obedient, and committed. Some old habits may be hard to break, but when you ask God to help you, he'll transform you to be what he created you to be.

I am giving you the key that unlocked the lock that had kept me bound for many years to drugs, prison, tobacco, alcohol, and bad relationships.

The key is the Jesus Factor. When I accepted God, he opened the door to freedom. Now I'm free from that bondage and free from sin, and it's only because I let Jesus in my life. Whether you are reading this book at a prison, jail, detention center, home, school, church, bus, train, car, hospital, nursing home, work, or at a hospice center, remember that Jesus loves you and he's waiting for you to call him. If you need help, just say this prayer:

> Father God, I know that I'm a sinner, and I repent from my wicked ways. I believe that Jesus died for my sins, was resurrected, and is living with you in heaven. I invite Jesus to come into my heart and transform my life. I also ask that the Holy Spirit guide my every move. I thank you, Father, and I receive your blessings in Jesus' name. Amen.

Welcome to God's family.

Now you can find a church in your area that believes in the full gospel of the Bible or contact us.

I thank God for allowing me to write this book. I give all the glory to God for all the things that he has done and is continuing to do in my life and in the lives of my family and friends. I also praise God for my pastor, Gilbert Silva, and all the ministers, people, and cell groups at House of Praise International Church in Lorain, Ohio.

To do the work of an evangelist, you must bring the Word of God to the lost. Help us bring the Word to many who are in need. Support us by buying our CD's, books, videos, and merchandise, but mainly support us with your prayers.

To send any of our books, videos, CD's, or merchandise to prisoners, you must get an authorization from the prison or we can send materials to our prison ministry members. Help us reach over one million prisoners in the United States. They may not pick up a Bible immediately, but they will pick up this book and read it because they can relate to it.

To get bulk quantities of this book, Brother Lew's CD's, tapes, videos, or other works, write to:

Lampara Music Group or Brother Lew Ministries
PO Box 674
Lorain, Ohio 44052

We sell bulk quantities of our books, tapes, videos and CD's to prevention and treatment organizations, church groups, prison ministries, missionaries, state and local correctional institutions, jails, juvenile detention facilities, hospitals, nursing homes, hospice centers, bookstores, retail outlets, the armed forces, and individuals who want to reach out to the lost, to the addicted, to the infirm, and to the imprisoned. We also drop ship pre-paid copies to any prison or facility that sends us approval. Ask for a copy of our brochure or check out our website at www.Lamparamusic.com or www.brother-lew.com.

Photo Album

Photo Album

Elena ready to go to church

Elena and Angel at Christmas

Josh at 8 years old

Angel at 14 years old

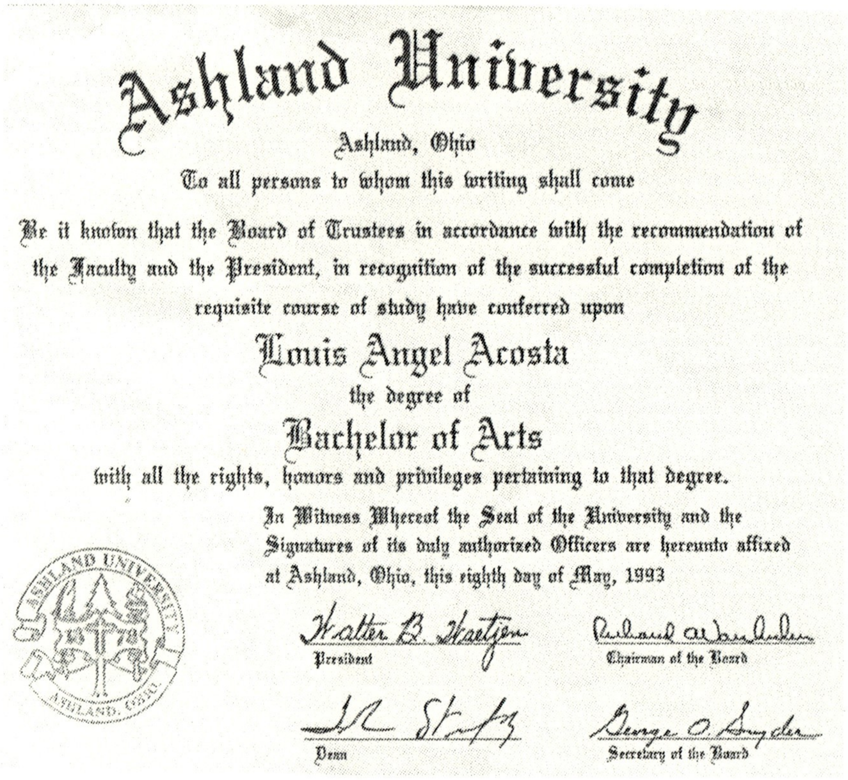

Ashland University

Ashland, Ohio

To all persons to whom this writing shall come

Be it known that the Board of Trustees in accordance with the recommendation of the Faculty and the President, in recognition of the successful completion of the requisite course of study have conferred upon

Louis Angel Acosta

the degree of

Bachelor of Arts

with all the rights, honors and privileges pertaining to that degree.

In Witness Whereof the Seal of the University and the Signatures of its duly authorized Officers are hereunto affixed at Ashland, Ohio, this eighth day of May, 1993

President

Chairman of the Board

Dean

Secretary of the Board

Bachelor's Degree from Ashland University

Photo Album

Two Associates Degrees from Fox Valley Technical Institute
One for Food Service Management and One for Restaurant and Hotel Cookery

Brother Lew

CHRISTIAN TELEVISION NETWORK
5565 Northland Drive • Suite 900 West • Southfield, Michigan 48075 • Business 810-559-4200 • FAX 810-559-575

December 30, 1997

Minister Lou Acosta
New Thing Ministries
3059 Palm Avenue
Lorain, OH 44055

Dear Lou:

Greetings in the precious name of our Lord and Savior, Jesus Christ!

"For in Him we live, move and have our being..." (Acts 17:28).

We trust that all is going well since you sacrificed time out of your busy schedule to so graciously accept the invitation to be our guest on Monday, December 29 28, 1997 on *CTN Live!*

There was great response to this telecast. This interview had a positive impact on our viewers and was quite encouraging to those who tuned in. The discussion was wonderful and you did a great job, touching multitudes with your thrilling testimony, insightful comments about youth and music among other things.

We pray for further success in your personal life and unique ministry of music throughout the world. Your love for God, joy in serving Him, and burden to reach the lost is so apparent. Stay humble and continue to give Him all the glory. Hopefully, we will get the pleasure of having you as a guest again soon!

Please pray for this network as we labor in this part of the vineyard. Be encouraged and steadfast in furthering His Kingdom. Keep in touch!

With warmest regards,

Glenn R. Plummer
President

GRP/fl

Appriciation letter for appearing on their show

Photo Album

GEORGE V. VOINOVICH
GOVERNOR

STATE OF OHIO
OFFICE OF THE GOVERNOR
COLUMBUS 43266-0601

June 20, 1997

Lou Acosta
1860 East 30th Street
Lorain, Ohio 44052

Dear Mr. Acosta:

I warmly invite you to attend an exciting event to be held at the Avenue at the Tower City Center - English Oak Room, 230 Huron Road N.W., in Cleveland on Wednesday, July 9, 1997. The Ohio Department of Rehabilitation and Correction (DRC), the Ohio Prison Fellowship and Forest City Management, Inc. are presenting, as a collaborative effort, an educational program focused on employing the many men and women who are exiting our prisons each day. The meeting will be held from 10:00 a.m. until 1:45 p.m. with lunch provided. Registration and coffee will begin at 9:30 a.m.

The program will brief you on the varied work, training and pre-release programs afforded those during incarceration. You will hear from employers who have given an ex-offender a second chance and have experienced the reward of converting a tax liability into a taxpaying, productive worker and citizen.

In this time of low unemployment, I know many of you are looking constantly for good workers. I would urge you to consider those coming from incarceration. This program will be very educational and informative for you, and it will introduce you to a process and procedure for examining the skills and talents of those returning to our communities from paying their debt to society.

If you plan to attend, please contact Ohio Prison Fellowship at 614-759-1571, by July 2, 1997. I look forward to seeing you on July 9th and the many others who will be attending this event.

Sincerely,

George V. Voinovich
Governor

The Governor's letter of invitation to Prison Fellowship Banquet

Me with my sisters Luisa and Isabel at the park after my first communion

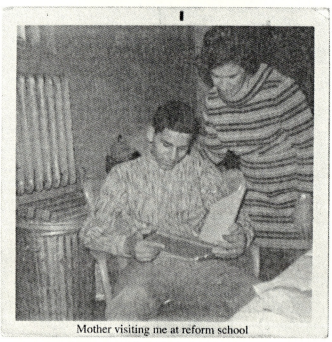

Mother visiting me at reform school

Photo Album

Me with Bob at Harvest Recording Studio

Me with Senator, (then Governor) George Voinovich

Plain Dealer story about my Rap Radio Program

Gospels go rap at Christian station

8-12-93

Just when you thought you had heard it all, Christian radio station WZLE-FM/104.9 is getting into rap.

At least it's doing so during the weekday midnight hours, courtesy of deejay "Brother Lou Acosta," a born-again Christian who is trying to lure listeners by spinning his own brand of hip-hop.

"What I play is gospel rap," says Acosta, 29, who eschews the Geto Boys and Ice Cube for more conservative beats on his show, "Gospel After Midnight." "When I go out in the community, kids are surprised by what they hear. They listen to it and some of them actually like it."

Gospel rap?

Instead of hearing MC Lyte belting out "Ruffneck," listeners hear Brother Lew and the Krew (Acosta's own group) dishing out "J.E.S.U.S."

Acosta's deejay grooves are strictly soul-, not rump-shaking.

"Gospel After Midnight," which blends Pentecostal rhetoric with urban vibes, is similar in spirit to last year's "Chuck and Jan Off The Wall," Christian station WRDZ-AM/1260's now-defunct morning show.

WRDZ believed that showcasing Christian virtues in a contemporary environment would attract listeners who ordinarily shun Christian radio. It didn't work for that station.

But Acosta thinks it has a chance at WZLE; he hopes the show will appeal to younger listeners than WRDZ attracted.

"Gospel After Midnight" is easy on the ears and manages to work. Acosta is an eclectic deejay, spinning gospel rap and Christian contemporary music when not reading from the Good Book. The execution at times comes across like a "Saturday Night Live" spoof, but it's the real McCoy.

Acosta says he doesn't know how many people tune in, but says that most are "shut-ins, the infirm, the imprisoned and those flicking

ROBERTO SANTIAGO

RADIO WAVES

through stations" mainly from Cleveland, Medina, Lorain, Akron and Sandusky.

"At first I didn't think anyone was listening, but after I started the call-in requests, I knew there was a very large market out there for ministr

"Free At Last" video available spring 2002

Photo Album

What is Gospel Rap the video.

Nearly dying changed ex-inmate's life

Cleveland Plain Dealer story one year after prison

Brother Lew

A Christian rocker
DJ loves radio job

By MOLLY CAVANAUGH
Morning Journal Correspondent

LORAIN — Christian radio disc jockey Lou Acosta was expecting a request for music when he took the call during his midnight-to-4 a.m. shift.

Instead, he listened as a woman sobbed in despair and threatened suicide.

Acosta, 39, quickly put on a long-playing compact disc of Christian music and prayed with the distraught mother.

After assuring his help, he called local counseling centers until he reached someone who could help.

"The morning hours are especially bad for some people," he said, "insomnia claims a lot of people. I've had it myself."

Acosta has an audience among second-, third-shift workers and people who don't sleep at night.

GOSPEL AIR — Lou Acosta of Lorain uses his talents as a musician and disc jockey to help folks who call his late-night show in Lorain. Here h reads from the Bible to a caller.

Lorain teens' lives

Lou Acosta of Lorain molded some of his own experiences into "Stop the Violence" to teach young people about finding peace through God.

The New York City native said that while serving a sentence at an Ohio prison on drug-related charges, he almost died of an overdose of painkillers. He said the trauma sparked his faith.

Acosta said he got the idea to produce the play with children from the House of Praise, where he is a member, after seeing the teens perform skits for the nondenominational Lorain church.

"The play developed from a secular play to a pure, Christian-oriented play, because of the influence of the kids," said the 43-year-old father of five.

Acosta, who supports prayer in schools, said teenagers need to see plays like "Stop the Violence," because those types of productions do not exist in high school.

"All they see is 'South Pacific' and 'Mary Poppins,'" he said. "We're talking about reality theater here. Everyone can relate to it."

Newspaper articles about accomplishments

Photo Album

Two crime buddies at reform school

Fox Valley Tech. Associate Degree Ceremony

playing
backgammon
in the
joint

with the brothers on the grounds at the federal prison

Photo Album

After Associates Degree Ceremony

My hispanic buddies at the federal prison

Brother Lew

* Community Corrections & Rehabilitation
* Alcoholism, Addiction & Mental Health Treatment
* Transitional Residence
* Shelter & Employment Assistance
* Pastoral Care & Support

THE SALVATION ARMY
Greater Cleveland Area Services
Harbor Light Complex
1710 Prospect Avenue Cleveland, Ohio 44115
Phone (216) 781-3773
Fax (216) 781-0870

John Gowans
General
Joe Noland
Territorial Commander
Major Charles R. Smith
Area Coordinator
John Ausbon, CSW
Executive Director, Harbor Light

December 4, 2001

To Whom It May Concern.

The purpose of this letter is to express appreciation for the services of Lou Acosta, who presents workshops for our clients under the outreach services of the Lorain County Alcohol and Drug Abuse Services, Inc.

Harbor Light Lorain is a residential chemical dependency treatment facility licensed by the State of Ohio as a halfway house. Our clients are men on probation or parole whose lives have been negatively affected by their involvement with drugs and/or alcohol. Many are substance abusers, many admit to chemical dependency.

Mr. Acosta has been faithfully coming to our facility weekly for the past two years in his role of prevention specialist. We acknowledge that some people think of "prevention" only in terms of those who have never used drugs or alcohol, but a recent publication on addiction affirms what we believe: that relapse may be the single most important issue in addiction. In this respect, Mr. Acosta provides a needed and much appreciated component of our recovery program. He is not only knowledgeable about his topic, but his manner of presentation is perfect for our population. He is upbeat and non-judgmental, and he has a good sense of humor, all excellent traits in an instructor. We hope that we may continue to include his presentations in our curriculum.

Sincerely,

Pat Strauss

Pat Strauss, Manager
Harbor Light Lorain

cc: file

Letter of appriciation from
Harbor Light Program

"Harbor Light...pioneering community services for over 50 years."
The Salvation Army is An Equal Opportunity Employer.
Harbor Light is partially funded by Ohio Department of Corrections & Rehabilitation, Ohio Department of Alcohol & Drug Addiction Services,
Cuyahoga County Community Mental Health Board, Cleveland Department of Community Development & The United Way.

Photo Album

To Whom It May Concern, January 12, 1999

The Elyria City Jail Has been involved with Mr. Louis Acosta of L.A.C.O.A. for the past several months. Mr. Acosta has provided an alcohol and drug awareness and education program to approximately thirty inmates during this time period. With the services he has provided, I have found the inmates that have been involved in this program have been less of a disciplinary problem and they are making a true effort at modifying their behavior inside this facility and also upon their release. I have personally observed three inmates make significant changes in their outlook on life and attribute this to what Mr. Acosta is doing in this program.

Mr. Acosta has made a definate impact in my jail operation and have found an increased number of inmates attending his program. If I can be of any further assistance please feel free to call me at 440-326-1328.

Regards,

Michael Gurich
Jail Administrator
Elyria City Jail

18 WEST AVENUE • ELYRIA OHIO 44035 • 440/326-1200 • FAX 440/326-1338

Letter of appriciation from the Elyria City Jail Administration

Brother Lew

OVER 100 People Come To The Lord After Viewing "Stop the Violence"

Over 100 people, decided to change their present lifestyles after viewing the real-life drama: "Stop the Violence" Tomorrow's not sure. In three shows, the attendance was over 1,350 people between the ages of 8 and 65 years of age. Students, teachers, professionals, counselors, heads of agencies, court officials clergy, and police officers were part of the audience. Drug addicts, juveniles, criminals, and gangmembers were among the converted. The play was written and directed by Lou Acosta and performed by the H.O.P. dramateam featuring songs by the Radical Fanatics GospelRap group. The play is about real life situations that are affecting our young people today : Drugs, Gangs, Aids, TeenSex, TeenPregnancy, Suicide, and Violence. Michelle Melendez, a reporter for the Plain Dealer wrote an article about the play. Robyn Roche, of WVIZ-TV asked for a copy of the video, and many are asking for the soundtracks of the songs. The dramateam is being invited to perform the drama at locations throughout Northeast Ohio. Recent plans include High School performances, an outdoor produced video and an audio cassette of the play. For information about the drama, performances, or tapes contact New Thing Drama Club P.O. Box 550 Lorain, Ohio 44052.

Newletter article about "Stop the Violence" play

Photo Album

Prevention presentation to youth

'Reality theater' dramatizes

By MICHELE M. MELENDEZ
PLAIN DEALER REPORTER

LORAIN — Despite her dismal view of the world, Celena Rodriguez has faith in her peers.

"There are so many things that are corrupt," said the 18-year-old Southview High School senior. "You go to the movies, and everything's corruption and violence. It's a perverse generation, but we're trying to put on something that's positive."

Religious images usually do not include gritty language, hip-hop clothes and rap music, but a play that highlights the flavor of Lorain street life has helped bring Rodriguez and about 30 other young performers closer to God.

The young group of House of Praise parishioners will perform "Stop the Violence: Tomorrow's Not Sure" tomorrow at Southview High School.

"A lot of times people think religion and church is boring and repetitious," said Admiral King High School senior Anthony Quintana, 18. "We have the rap music and the acting, applying our God to almost any situation, from gangs to AIDS."

Plain Dealer article about "Stop the Violence" play

7 Arrested, 15 Pounds of Heroin and Cocaine Seized

By JILL SMOLOWE

More than $1 million worth of uncut heroin was seized and seven men were arrested Wednesday in connection with an international heroin distribution operation, drug-enforcement officials said.

Bail for six of the suspects was set yesterday, ranging from $20,000 to $3 million. The seventh man was released after a United States Magistrate, Nina Gershon, found that the complaint against him had been improperly prepared.

The investigation involved more than 65 agents, making it one of the largest inquiries in New York in recent years, said James Judge, a spokesman for the Drug Enforcement Administration. In addition to seizing the heroin, which weighed nine pounds, he said, agents also confiscated six pounds of cocaine worth $180,000 and five weapons.

Those arrested included Sal Sferrazza, 57 years old, of 22-61 23d Street, Anthony Todisco, 38, of 149-54 21st Avenue, and David D'Angelo, 37, of 8-05 162d Street, all in Queens; Anthony Vallone, 38, of 48 Summit Avenue, Hector Torres, 49, of 1226 Boynton Avenue, and Luis Acosta, 27, of 2830 Sedgwick Avenue, all in the Bronx. The seventh suspect, John Compopiano, 46, of 29 Fieldcrest Road in Queens was released. The bail of $3 million was set on Mr. Sferrazza. Bail of $1 million each was set on Mr. Todisco and Mr. Vallone.

More Arrests Expected

The arrests grew out of an investigation begun in April by the New York office of the Drug Enforcement Administration and the office of the United States Attorney for the Southern District in New York. These were the first arrests in the investigation and more are anticipated, Mr. Judge said.

The New York inquiry is part of a larger investigation that was initiated in March by the Drug Enforcement Administration encompassing Baltimore, Boston, Newark, Philadelphia, and Washington. Drug enforcement officials said they were investigating possible connections between heroin operations in each of these cities, which have been hit hard since 1978 by quantities of heroin smuggled in from Iran, Pakistan and Afghanistan.

In another drug case yesterday, three men and a woman were arrested in Manhattan on charges of heroin and cocaine possession. The police said they seized 11,000 bags of heroin worth $110,000 and one ounce of uncut cocaine and 500 bags of cut cocaine worth $20,000 at 162 East Second Street, where the four were arrested at 9 A.M.

The police said a fifth suspect escaped from the apartment before the arrests were made.

New York Times article on big bust in New York City

*****

What is a Christian Rapper? A rapper who is christian or a christian who is a rapper. What do rappers put emphasis on, the rapping or the lifestyle. Rappers claiming to be true to hip hop must be aware of what they are saying. Some rappers ruin their testimonies by stating that they'll be true to hip hop til they die. That's contradicting the true goals of a Gospel or Christian rapper. Christian is the lifestyle that you chose to live, the Gospel is the word that you chose to obey, and rap is only a form used in delivering the word. When you don't use the word then it's not Christian or Gospel Rap. **Jesus must be the focus of your ministry..**

Reprint of my article on Christian rap

Printed in the United States
855100003B